HOW SLEEP THE BRAVE

Remembering those who gave their all for freedom

To the families of the Brave.
We can't thank you or the Brave enough but we are teaching our children.

How Sleep the Brave: Remembering Those Who Gave Their All for Freedom

Written by Lindsey Michaels
Introduction by Christopher Flannery
How Sleep the Brave poem written by William Collins in 1746

Copyright © 2023 by Lindsey Michaels
ISBN 979-8-9881864-1-0

All rights reserved. No portion of this book may be used or reproduced in any matter whatsoever without written permission from the publisher. For permissions contact:

Lmichaelsbooks@gmail.com

HOW SLEEP THE BRAVE

Remembering those who gave their all for freedom

LINDSEY MICHAELS   Poem by WILLIAM COLLINS   Introduction by CHRISTOPHER FLANNERY

INTRODUCTION

Abigail Adams quoted from memory this ode by English poet William Collins in a letter to her husband John, mailed on Tuesday, June 20, 1775. She had just confirmed reports of the death of their dear friend and family doctor, 34-year-old Joseph Warren. He had fallen "gloriously fighting for his Country," Abigail wrote, and "Those favorite lines of Collin[s] continually sound in my Ears."

* * *

Back in that spring and summer of 1775, when he was just seven years old and the War for Independence swirled around him and his family, John Quincy Adams remembered, "[my mother] taught me to repeat daily after the Lord's prayer [the Ode of Collins] before rising from bed."

Christopher Flannery
The American Story podcast

John was seven years old when his mother took him outside to watch the Battle of Bunker Hill.

From a distance they could hear the guns and cannons and see the smoke and fighting. John's dad was out of town in Philadelphia and everything was scary.

John's mother chose not to hide. She brought him to watch. She wanted him to see what was happening and know what brave people were doing *for him*.

She wanted him to always remember.

John's mother is Abigail Adams and she taught him a poem called *How Sleep the Brave*. She had it memorized and he memorized it, too. It taught him to always remember the Brave because of what they gave for him. They gave everything they had for him and all of us, for freedom.

We can't thank each one, but we can always remember what they did.

Grave of Dr. Joseph Warren and family
Massachusetts, USA

*How sleep the brave,
who sink to rest*

Boston Massacre and Christopher Snider (Seider) grave marker
Massachusetts, USA

By all their country's wishes blest!

*When Spring,
with dewy fingers cold,*

Arlington National Cemetery
Virginia, USA

*Returns to deck
their hallow'd mould,*

Manila American Cemetery
The Philippines

*She there shall dress
a sweeter sod*

Normandy American Cemetery and Memorial overlooking Omaha Beach
France

*Than Fancy's feet
have ever trod.*

USS Arizona Memorial, Pearl Harbor in Oahu
Hawaii, USA

*By fairy hands
their knell is rung;*

North Africa American Cemetery and Memorial
Tunisia

*By forms unseen
their dirge is sung;*

Gettysburg National Cemetery
Pennsylvania, USA

*There Honour comes,
a pilgrim grey,*

Cambridge American Cemetery and Memorial
England

*To bless the turf
that wraps their clay;*

And Freedom shall awhile repair

*To dwell,
a weeping hermit, there!*

GLOSSARY

deck – decorate

hallow'd – holy, sacred; short for *hallowed*

mould – shape; in the USA we spell it *mold*

sod – ground, usually with grass on it

trod – walked, stepped

knell – the sound from a bell with a slow, sad ring, announcing a death or funeral

dirge – a very sad song played or sung because someone has died

pilgrim – traveler coming to a very special place

turf – ground, usually made with grass and roots

repair – restore, strengthen, make it good

hermit – someone who chooses to go somewhere without a lot of people around

Glossary words are usually listed alphabetically but the words here are in the order they are found in William Collins' poem to make it easier for a young reader to use.

Listen to Christopher Flannery's full episode *How Sleep the Brave* at theamericanstorypodcast.org.

The American Story is a production by Chris Flannery of the Claremont Institute.

PHOTO CREDITS:

Grave of Dr. Joseph Warren and family photo courtesy of Jake Sconyers of the HUB History podcast.

Boston Massacre grave marker Photo courtesy of Erwin Bernal.

Sicily-Rome American Cemetery, Nettuno, Italy. ABMC Photo by Don Savage.

Normandy American Cemetery and Memorial Overlooking Omaha Beach Photo credit: Jrwadf1435 This file is licensed under the Creative Commons Attribution-Share Alike 4.0 International license.

USS Arizona Memorial photo by: PH3(AW/SW) JAYME PASTORIC, USN.

Gettysburg National Cemetery photo by Henryhartley.

All other photos are in the public domain, including those found at arlingtoncemetery.mil and canva.com.